I AM
NEW ONE

I AM NEW ONE

By
Mary Michael Isaac

Published by:
The Riehle Foundation
P.O. Box 7
Milford, OH 45150

Published by The Riehle Foundation

The publisher recognizes and accepts that the final authority regarding the authenticty of apparitions at Medjugorje rests with the Holy See of Rome, to whose judgment we willingly submit.
—The Publisher

Individuals wishing to obtain additional copies of this book should contact:
>   The Riehle Foundation
>   P.O. Box 7
>   Milford, Ohio 45150
>   1-513-576-0032

Bookstores and book distributors should contact:
>   Faith Publishing Company
>   P.O. Box 237
>   Milford, Ohio 45150
>   1-513-576-6400

Copyright © 1994, Mary Michael Isaac

Library of Congress Catalog Card No.: 94-069104

ISBN: 1-877678-32-5

Printed in The United States

All rights reserved. No part of this book may be reproduced or transmitted in any form whatsoever without the expressed permission of the publisher. For information, contact, The Riehle Foundation, P.O. Box 7, Milford, Ohio 45150.

Contents

Dedication vii

Preface ix

Chapter 1—Before and After 1

Chapter 2—Turning Point 6

Chapter 3—Increasing Pain 12

Chapter 4—To Have And To Hold 16

Chapter 5—The Darkness Creeps In 21

Chapter 6—Blackouts 26

Chapter 7—Intervention Day 29

Chapter 8—The First Step—Surrender! 32

Chapter 9—The Disease Screams 36

Chapter 10—Another Test 44

Chapter 11—I Have Learned 51

Chapter 12—And The Grace Flowed 55

Chapter 13—Prayer From The Heart 67

Chapter 14—I Am New One 75

Epilogue 78

Message 81

Credits 83

Dedication

Dedicated with love and gratitude to Our Lady, Queen of Peace.

Special thanks to my husband for his love and steadfast support.

Preface

My real name is not Mary Michael Isaac.

I chose the name Mary in honor of the Blessed Virgin Mary and also in honor of St. Mary Magdalene (Mary Magdalene was possessed with SEVEN devils and yet the Lord loved her—so much so that she was the first one to see Him on Easter Sunday morning).

I chose the name Michael in honor of St. Michael the Archangel. May he ever this day be at my side, to light, to guard, to rule and to guide.

I chose the name Isaac in honor of a shepherd—a faithful and faithfilled follower of Jesus of Nazareth.

Abortion is a major problem in our world. And who is not aware of the ravages and destruction caused by alcoholism and other forms of chemical dependency? Ultimately, and finally, the Lord becomes the only solution. That's called conversion. It seems like the world is in desperate need of it.

I have been blessed to have experienced all of these issues. Perhaps it is time for me to tell my story. Perhaps it can truly help a number of others. Perhaps that is part of the conversion process.

Chapter 1

Before and After

I have been thinking so much lately about turning points. There seem to be major times in our lives when the choices we make are so vitally important. I have had a few very major turning points in my life. I wonder if this is true for everyone?

In the Fall of 1983, I felt I had reached a pinnacle of happiness in my life. I was married to a wonderful man, had a wonderful family and lots of friends. I was living a lifestyle I had always wanted. Then one day my whole world changed, and things have never been the same. I can divide my life into the "before" and "after." Let me share what happened.

I have a wonderful family. Memories of my childhood are filled with love and happiness. I have one younger brother and a large family of aunts, uncles and cousins.

My mother's family is from Kentucky. Some of the best summers of my life were spent at my grandmother's home in Vine Grove, Kentucky. My Grandmother was a legend in this little town. She was a mid-wife, a nurse, a pioneer who serviced many of the sick and needy.

My father was a twin. He and his brother were incredibly close and they had a tremendous influence on my growing up. The two of them were outgoing, aggressive, fun, loving, and competitive. They loved one another and their families fiercely. All that has ever been said or written about twins I saw first hand to be true. There is a bond that is very special. The example of their love and warmth was a joy to be around. Early memories of my dad are of him up at the crack of dawn on the weekends pacing the floor until tee time for a round of golf with his brother and their friends. I was surrounded by love and warmth.

My brother and I attended Catholic schools. The Franciscan Sisters were very dedicated and very strict. I was a good little girl and strived to be perfect. Life was good.

I guess it was when I was in sixth grade that I began to sense a change—there was something wrong in our house. The rhythm was off. Late at night I could hear the tempo and tone of my parents conversation come to a different pitch than any I had heard before. It wasn't long before I could put together a direct connection between the harsh words and the bottle of Echo Springs left out on the kitchen counter. No matter how hard I pressed the pillow over my ears, I couldn't shut out the sound of the quarreling.

Always, in the morning, things were sunshine and normal. So normal, I often thought I had just had bad dreams. The episodes worsened and gradually my dad, this handsome, fun, great guy spiraled his way to being a full blown "practicing" alcoholic. Oh, I didn't know then to put that label on him. I just knew if he had "that look" in his eyes, we were in for a real nasty night. I quickly learned not to have friends over. Everyone was very good at pretending all was well. No one ever mentioned a word about dad's drinking—but both my brother and I seethed with anger.

All of this was very confusing. I loved dad a lot. He was such a great guy and a super father. But I also hated his guts. I told him off in my mind so many times. My anger was so intense it overwhelmed me on occasion. He was hateful and I was afraid. I would fantasize about the nasty things I could say or do to him while all the time presenting a happy-go-lucky face to the world. One thing I knew for sure—I would never be like him.

The year I graduated from high school dad's brother died suddenly in the middle of the night of a massive heart attack. He was 44. My Uncle was the "good twin," the steady one whose eyes never got glassy. Our entire family was in shock. A big part of my dad died that night too; he was never the same after his brother's death. Dad drank more and more and sank deeper into depression.

And for me? I escaped this unhappiness by getting married. My husband was a nice person. We were young and naive and things seemed good. We had a beautiful daughter, Carolyn Marie. Carolyn was the joy of my life—so beautiful. I vowed to be a perfect mother to her and never let her experience the unhappiness I had known at the hands of my father.

I became pregnant with my second child when Carolyn was three years old. One morning my brother-in-law came to our door and told me my dad had died in the middle of the night of a massive heart attack. It had been three years since his brother had died. In those three years not one day had passed that dad had not grieved for him. In fact, it became an obsession as he constantly told us: "Our bodies are identical, I will die just like he did." He lived in constant fear of the "big one" and we all got so tired of his using this as an excuse to drink. I would scream inside my head: "So why don't you just shut up and die then!"

Then he did die—just like he had known he would. I was filled with guilt and shame—and anger. How I loved him! How I hated him!

Our family gathered once again around a coffin—looking at the identical body of the twin we had buried three years earlier. Our hearts were breaking. So young, so tortured, and so troubled. It was very confusing.

My second daughter, Beth, was born three months after my Dad died. She was two months premature, but a spunky little thing with a strong personality.

Shortly after Beth was born things went badly for my husband and me and we were separated, and then divorced. It was a sad time. We still cared for one another, but for a variety of reasons, we could not and did not stay together.

I found myself a single parent and things were difficult for a while. I credit my two darling girls for keeping me sane during this troubled and insecure time. I had to be strong for them.

Chapter 2

Turning Point

Several years passed as I raised my girls and tried to make a nice life for them and for myself. In 1977, I met a man who was soon to become my husband. Bud was gentle and quiet, and I recognized a strength of character in him that was very special.

Being with Bud opened up a new world for me. He had a beautiful boat and belonged to a yacht club. We spent many hours on the water, relaxing and partying with a wide circle of friends. My family loved Bud, too. My daughters loved him—we knew he was special.

When our thoughts turned to marriage, Bud and I both realized that the Catholic faith we had both been raised in was still a big part of who we were. We wanted very much to be married in the Church. We decided to go through the annulment process. The counseling for this annulment was very intense. We both were forced to do a lot of soul-searching and looking into our past lives. We both had to face a lot of hurt from our past. By facing up to and

TURNING POINT

understanding the mistakes we had made, we learned a lot about ourselves and one another. It was a terrific preparation for marriage.

We were both very happy when our annulments were granted. We were married in the Church and our love of God, of the Church and the sacraments grew. Bud and I were very close. We really had a good marriage. My girls were terrific. Those first years of marriage were wonderful! We traveled some, enjoyed our boat, and a warm loving home. Life was good.

One day in September of 1983, Carolyn and I were driving to the mall for a little shopping. In the car she turned and dropped a bombshell on me that changed my life forever. She turned and said: "Mom, I'm pregnant." I felt the blood drain from my face and I asked "How long?" When she told me five months, I nearly wrecked the car. I absolutely lost it. In fact, I have gauged my life since that day as the "before" and "after." Even my husband says to this day—I am not the same person he married. Something in me changed forever that day.

How could this have happened? Why hadn't I seen this coming? We are so close, Carolyn and I. How could I have been so blind? How could I have been such a dummy? How could I have been such a rotten mother?

The very first thought that came into my mind was: "OK, she needs me now. I can handle this. I know just what to do. We can get rid of this problem and no one will ever have to know." I rushed home and immediately got on the phone to make arrangements for an abortion at the clinic here in town. They told me over the phone that Carolyn was too far along for them to handle and they referred me to an abortion clinic near Detroit, Michigan, where they do late abortions—right up to the ninth month, if necessary. This was a Friday, so I made an appointment for the next Monday. That was such a terrible weekend. I called my friend, Paula, and she agreed to come along with us for the drive—for moral support.

It was ironic that Paula was the friend I chose to go with us. She and her husband had been trying for years to have a baby. She did not believe in abortion. Well, neither did I. I'm a Catholic, after all, and the Catholic Church is against abortion. Well, so am I—but this case was different! Carolyn was 14 years old!

Monday came and I spent the entire drive to that clinic praying. I knew the action we were about to take was wrong, but I had no choice. Carolyn was so young and this was so awful for her. I was still in a state of shock. On the drive up to Detroit I asked Carolyn why she had not come to me sooner. She told me, "because I thought it would go away." So, now she needed me—we were going to face this through together. I prayed for the courage I knew we would both need.

"As for me, I'll cry tomorrow. I'll come to terms with this later. I know this is a sin, but God understands. I know He will forgive me. I will have to beg for His forgiveness, and it will be hard, and I will feel some guilt, but for now, I will put those God-thoughts out of my head and get this problem taken care of. It would be so embarrassing if our friends found out. How would we ever tell our family? I'll pray tomorrow. For now, God, please, help me get through this." I was traumatized inside and I cried like I had never cried before. I was so afraid, and I called out to the dear Lord to help me.

Have you ever been inside an abortion clinic? I certainly had not, and had never given any thought at all what it would be like to enter one.

When Paula, Carolyn and I got to the clinic we went inside and sat in the waiting room. This was an intense place. Several young girls were sitting there. Some were alone, some were with a parent. No one looked at anyone else, in fact everyone had their eyes trained on the floor. The whole place was very clean and orderly, with gentle music playing in the room. The nurses were great—very friendly and caring. They put us at ease right away.

I was called back into the treatment room with Carolyn. The doctor came in—such a nice man. He was tall, dark, good-looking and very reassuring. He was dark-skinned and spoke with a beautiful Spanish accent. He called Carolyn his "little Caroleena" and he began what I can only describe as a "sing-song." He told us what a good thing we were doing. After all, Carolyn had her whole life ahead of her, she deserved a chance to have fun, finish high school, have dates, enjoy a normal teenage experience. The doctor also included me in his advice. I didn't need to be burdened at this time in my life. I had a right to a little freedom, a chance to enjoy life with my husband. Carolyn and I sat and nodded. It felt so good to know we were doing the right thing.

We helped Carolyn undress and she climbed up on the table. She looked so young and vulnerable—I had a huge lump in my throat. It was shocking to see how big the bulge in her tummy was. She had been wearing skin-tight jeans to hide her condition. I said a heart-felt prayer for the success of this procedure. Carolyn seemed so darn little for this big thing to come out of. The nurse rolled in a machine for an ultrasound so they could observe what they were doing. The nurse was standing by Carolyn as the doctor prepped her.

They forgot about me.

I saw a little face come into focus. I could see a little fist and tiny clenched eyes. The room grew totally silent. What were they going to do to this tiny little face floating there so quietly? I felt a warm rush go through my body.

I started to laugh. A bright light filled the room that I could see and feel. I was suddenly filled with joy. The nurse and the doctor thought I had lost it. They tried to calm me down but I just threw Carolyn's clothes at her and shouted "Get up! We're going home! We are not doing this!"

I was like a crazy person. I did have to stop at the desk on the way out and pay them $74.00 for services rendered.

Paula had been waiting for us in that bleak waiting

room. She told us on the way home that she couldn't understand it when we walked out. She thought the abortion had taken place and she couldn't believe how I was just beaming!

Chapter 3

Increasing Pain

I knew I had made the right decision. There was a deep warmth within me—a knowing.

But, I was now faced with a 14 year old daughter, pregnant, a sophomore in high school.

It was very difficult to let people know of this situation. Each person I told was a trauma—my mother, my brother, the rest of the family. My husband was a rock of strength. My youngest daughter took the news very hard and I had blurted it out when I told her—handling things very badly.

Foremost in my mind was the thought that no matter what, Carolyn was going to finish high school. She was a good student and I knew an education was vital to her future. I met with the counselors at the high school. I had considered sending Carolyn to a different school to help her avoid embarrassment among her classmates. (Silly me. They already knew. I was one of the last to know. How blind and dumb I was. My hurt was matched only by an inner anger I felt at the injustice of all this.)

INCREASING PAIN

I could tell the counselors at school were very indifferent to my problem. I was dying inside and they seemed so cold. Finally the dean told me "Carolyn is one of seven girls in the sophomore class who is pregant." Six others! Were six other mothers going through the same turmoil I was? How were they coping? What were they doing? Did they feel the same searing pain inside that I did?

The decision was made to let Carolyn continue at the same school. One of the hardest days of my life was when Carolyn put on her first maternity outfit and headed off for school. I watched from the window as she walked across the front lawn, carrying her school books, wearing her tennis shoes, with her big big belly, and climb up onto that school bus. I doubled over with pain. I was surprised at how much this physically hurt me. I was awash with guilt and feelings of contempt for myself. My heart ached for this gorgeous child who had no idea what she had done.

Every day brought new pain. We could feel the baby move and kick inside Carolyn. She would come to my bed at night and we could feel the baby move and the pain in me would cut like a knife. It would not go away—it was always there.

As friends found out about this situation, I found out just how different people are, and how strong opinions are on this idea of teen pregnancy. This was 1983 and instead of being something to be ashamed of—it was merely something to get rid of.

Close friends, who had children of their own,

really admonished me. They told me how wrong I was to let this continue. One friend told me she would go with us to Detroit Memorial Hospital where abortions are done into the ninth month, and that I had no right to do this to my husband, to my daughter, to myself. Many of these arguments made sense to me and they made me feel so guilty—like I had been a coward not to just let them take this baby.

Day after day my turmoil increased. Each morning I woke up with a constant, screaming pain in my stomach. Sleep was nearly impossible. I was up and down throughout the night, stewing and worrying about what to do, what would happen next—what about Carolyn, what about me?

I have always prided myself in being a strong and reliable person. I still put on a good act of being in control. No one knew it; they thought I was handling things so well—but I was dying inside. My life was just whirling out of control and I will never know why this threw me so badly. I was a walking nervous breakdown.

My husband would take me out and as people talked and visited, as the band played and laughter swirled around me, I wanted to scream. I felt so isolated and alone. I knew when I got home I would have to go into Carolyn's room and say goodnight to that tiny girl with the huge belly and feel hurt again.

I quickly learned a very important lesson—I was a VERY convincing actress. If I was very careful, no one saw my mask slip, they couldn't see the hurt.

Life for Carolyn and me became a whirl of lamaze and counseling classes. Counselors pushed very hard for adoption. It seemed like a good solution.

Chapter 4

To Have And To Hold

Lamaze classes were very awkward. There were a lot of happy couples, but also a few mothers with their daughters. They seemed so together and happy. One time I did see my own pain reflected back to me in another mother's face, but we quickly looked away—embarrassed by what we had let show.

Christmas that year was a very confusing time for our family. Caroly was now eight months pregnant. She wanted posters, records and pretty clothes. She needed maternity jeans and tops.

Friday, February 9th, Carolyn came home from a full day of school exhausted and haggard looking. During dinner, her water broke and we rushed her to the hospital. I had agonized over this moment. I put on a gown and went into the labor room. As Carolyn's lamaze coach, I could be with her every step of the way. I was so afraid for her. Actually, she had a very easy labor. And, as much as I love Carolyn, a part of me was disappointed it was so easy. I had hoped it would hurt, be tough on her,

TO HAVE AND TO HOLD

show her just how serious this whole situation was, to realize the enormity of what she had done! I was angry she wasn't feeling remorse!

As we wheeled Carolyn into the delivery room—nothing seemed real. As the baby came—I watched Carolyn's face and saw her light up with joy as she heard the baby's first cry. This little child who tumbled out into the doctor's hands was so beautiful. The doctor handed her to me and I put a little cap on her head to keep her warm. I had never seen anything so incredible.

I sat holding this little one and tried to memorize every detail of her face. I said aloud "Will you ever forgive me for giving you away? They say you should be put up for adoption. Will I know you if I see you in a few years? What will become of you?" My thoughts flashed back to that moment in the abortion clinic when I had seen this little face on the ultrasound screen. I was so grateful for God's having spared this little one. She seemed so very special. Her hair was so blonde (she reminded me so much of how Carolyn had looked when she was born). I wondered if every other mother or grandmother had felt this way. I knew of no one who had gone through this, and I felt empty of all but pain.

That night after returning home, I could not sleep and could not get that little face out of my mind. The next day, in Carolyn's room, several members of the family came to visit. I watched as my mother came into the room and held this little girl. She held her for a long time, rocking her, talking to her, loving her. I thought back to seeing her hold Carolyn this same way. I imagine it's how she had looked when she held me.

We brought Carolyn home and left that child in the hospital to go to a foster home temporarily. No papers had been signed, so we were told to go home and think about it. At home, I just fell apart. This was my own flesh and blood. There would never be another child like this one. I will never be able to put into words the bond I felt with this child. I had pulled her from that abortion clinic only to give her away!

My mother came to me and offered to take her away and raise her. Family members told me, give her up, keep her, I was torn apart. One afternoon I was walking by a picture of my dad. I looked at that picture and thought: "Wonder what you would say if you were here." I knew the answers before I had finished the sentence. He would say "she's family—keep her." It was about one hour later that my husband came to me and said: "You might just as well go out and buy some baby clothes because there is no way you are not going to keep that baby."

Bud's support was the deciding factor for me. I called the foster family and told them of our decision. At seven days—our Stephanie came home.

I would love to tell you that we all lived happily ever after.

How I loved this little girl! She was so beautiful with soft clean baby smells. I melted each time I held her and said a prayer of thanks to God for sparing her, and sparing me. I knew this choice had been turned over to me from the moment Carolyn told me she was pregnant. She took the entire burden and put it on me—because she was my child and, as a mother, that's just how it is!

It was so strange though, showing my 15 year old daughter how to change, feed and care for her own baby. Beth, who was eleven years old, had to adjust to a niece. And we all had to adjust to having a baby in the house.

It surprised me how much pain was still left. I thought going through the pregnancy and birth would be the hardest part. I wasn't prepared for the searing pain that was on-going. It was hard to discipline Carolyn—to handle school, friends, dating and staying out with her friends. I was torn between wanting her to have a normal, happy high school life and wanting her to face up to what she had done, to be an adult, be responsible, be a mother. Life around our house, while filled with love, was also very confusing and intense. It was hard to separate the woman from the teenager, from the daughter, from the mother, from the sister.

I was learning to perfect my acting skills. I smiled a lot and never let my mask slip. And I found a way to ease a lot of the pain. I started to drink.

Now, this really helped me! Through social activities and boating I had always drank socially. But, I was careful not to have too much and become "unladylike." I would think of my dad and be so filled with disgust. It kept me very careful.

But now I learned that a glass of wine before bed made me feel very mellow and sleep came easier. Also, when I came home from work, a glass or two of wine relaxed me and made doing all I had to do so much easier. It also made me feel warm and loving toward Bud, my girls, and the baby. It really eased the pain.

Friends (well meaning, dear friends), would still comment to me—"what about Carolyn's future—this choice will ruin her life—what about giving her a chance—what about Bud, he didn't count on this when he married you? And a drink or two would ease the pain.

I knew the choice was a good one though, whenever I would look at Stephanie—so pure and so sweet. She brought a lot of happiness to our household—and of course all the work and fun involved with having a baby. But each time I looked at her, a slice of pain would shoot through me as I saw myself hell-bent for Michigan and for that abortion clinic. I felt so guilty—appalled at what I had almost done. If I had gone through with that killing, I would never know this little beauty, stealing our hearts and showing us such unconditional love.

Stephanie called me NEW ONE—right from the start. I don't know why—maybe as opposed to Old One! But to this day, that's who I am. *I am New One,* and I like it!

Chapter 5

The Darkness Creeps In

I tried to be a good wife, a good mother, a good grandma, a good friend, a good worker. I perfected my act each day, and of course, I always had a drink or two as a way to relax. I began to look forward to my "break."

I was still very careful, just as I had been all my life. NO WAY was I ever going to be like my dad—NEVER!

As time went by, it occurred to me just how much drinking helped me. It was something I could take or leave, but something I could really enjoy. There were still fun times on the boat and trips to Put-In-Bay. I enjoyed being on the boat on hot summer days, sipping a cold glass of wine or a tall cool drink.

As I look back now, I realize there was a darkness slowly creeping in. This was like a soft shadow, a gradual, slow, slow spiral.

Stephanie grew—smart and gorgeous. Carolyn completed high school and Beth entered high school. Life moved on. There was a slight haze beginning to form over everything, a film that can only be understood if you have been there. My pattern was erratic at first—drinking a bit—pulling back—smiling and having a "good time."

I really loved my husband, my daughters, my family. My life was filled with a lot of activities and friends. And, if occassionally I had a little too much to drink, well, I was just a good time girl who likes to party. I liked to have fun! If it seemed like anyone was in the least little bit upset with me, I would just act extra sweet and loving. The nicer I was to my family, the more I bought for them or did for them, the less likely they would be to think about my "silliness" the night before. Then, what I did privately could still remain my own business.

Without my ever telling them, my family learned NEVER to mention my drinking. And by never mentioning it—it went away, and I never had to worry that they would see my dark side.

I learned how much I could drink without my words beginning to slur (a real giveaway). I knew drinking was not a problem or anything for me, and I didn't want anyone insinuating that it was. After all, they didn't know how I felt inside and this was my life, not theirs.

My life was fine. I did have a nagging problem though, and that was how to hide those bottles. I resented the fact that I even had to hide them. Sometimes I wanted to just let the bottle sit out and pour from it for an evening cocktail; but I knew that might open the way for someone to say something negative or insulting (so what they didn't know wouldn't hurt them). I did a lot of hiding.

I was very careful. I never drank during the day. But when evening came, I began taking sips right out of the bottle I now carried with me in my purse. It took many months to get to this point, a slow creepy spiral, and I did not see what was happening to me. I just knew it made life more gentle and safe.

The darkness deepened.

What a phony I was. It's one thing to be a hypocrite and not be aware of the pardox between your thoughts and your actions. But I was a phony and I *knew* it. Always in my mind was that next bottle—how to get it—how to hide it—how to get *to* it.

Throughout the course of each day I would think about how I was NOT going to drink again. But towards the end of the afternoon I would be on fire and the decision to go ahead anyway, just for this one more evening, brought a sense of overwhelming relief and I must say, happiness. I wouldn't have too much—just enough to relax. And with the decision made to stop and buy the little pint, I could relax!

I began to avoid mirrors. I became grossly ugly. Yet, the creature staring back at me wasn't me, not really. How did this happen to me? It just wasn't fair!

One day while watching the Phil Donahue show, someone mentioned the most wonderful thing. Vodka leaves no smell. That was such a happy day for me. At last I realized I could totally hide any drinking I might occassionally want to do and no one would be disturbed. So, I began stopping at the State Liquor Store. Vodka is sold by the pint—tiny little bottles that were easy to keep quiet—to myself. And, best of all, a little went a long way, so I could really cut down. What a relief. I had begun to be afraid I was a "wino" or something. No, I was still a lady, and I began to feel like one again.

My daughter Beth graduated from high school. Carolyn got married one year later and had another girl, Jessica. A little doll! Carolyn's family was complete, a beautiful blessing. Both little ones called me *"New One"*—sometimes *"Newie."* I loved them so much! All these milestones! Life was good.

And the darkness was deepening.

When I would catch myself eye to eye in the mirror, I would toast myself and my dad: "Here's to you Dad. I'm just like you were—a chip off the old block, as they say. And I hate me more than I ever hated you!"

I can recall being overcome with ANGER. I would be driving alone in the car screaming vile obscenities at the top of my lungs until my throat was raw and hoarse. I couldn't believe the words or the ugly sounds that came out of me. I was just so MAD. And I don't even know what I was mad at, but it sure was strong! In those moments I could have ripped someone to shreds—physically or verbally, maybe both. I cringe to remember I was usually driving a car when this happened, racing to get to the liquor store before it closed!

Again, my acting talents paid off. To "the world" I showed a sweet face. Boy! Did I have them fooled. They would cringe in hate at my ugliness if they saw the real me.

On Sunday mornings in Church, I would go to communion and apologize to God over and over for bringing Him in to my black pit. I would pray to God to please help me stop this. My husband and kids were becoming so disgusted with me (I could see it in their eyes). Help me! I promise I'll be good.

I often could smell the fumes from the night before just oozing out of me. Just the sight of myself in the glass of the church doors made me want to throw up! I would promise God over and over—deep in my heart—and I truly meant it—I would never drink EVER AGAIN.

Chapter 6

Blackouts

I remember the first time I questioned my sanity. I woke up one morning fully dressed under the covers—shoes and all. For the life of me I could not remember climbing into bed. My husband made no comment. I thought, "I must have been really tired."

The next strange occurrence was when I woke one morning really hungry. I went down to the kitchen and saw my place still set from the night before. I guess I had forgotten to eat. I wondered, "What did I fix? Did anyone else eat?"

A few days later, my husband asked me some questions about where I had put some papers he needed. I could not remember. He became very angry and made a very rude comment about drinking. And I thought, "to hell with him, he's got a nerve!"

But, that's when it hit me. I must have been having a blackout! I had heard of that, but is that what it meant?

These blackouts were awful and began happening

on a regular basis. I would have conversations with people and not remember what was said. I began to cover my tracks. I had a pencil and paper with me at all times so I could jot down who I was talking to, and a bit of what we were talking about. This note taking became really important with phone calls. I was embarrassed though, to find out that many times when I went back to refer to my notes, I could not read a word. It was awful, so I stopped taking notes.

One evening Bud and I went to dinner and ran into some good friends. They are an older couple whom we had not seen in several months. I knew they had a grandaughter who had leukemia. We asked how the little one was, and they told us she had died. We sat for a long time talking and sharing with them. The poor grandma was heartbroken. We cried, and prayed. She shared her brokenness with me, and I held her hand and hurt with her. We hugged one another as we parted and said how blessed we were to have friends to share with.

Two weeks later, at a party, we ran into this same couple. I asked her "How's your little grandaughter doing these days?"

I will never forget the look on her face. I will never forget the look on my husband's face. He was so angry! She was so upset! My husband reminded me of our meeting with them two weeks before, and he told me about the sharing and caring. I realized I had been in a blackout the entire time my friend had been sharing her grief with me.

This whole incident really threw me. I was humiliated and I was scared. I felt I was really a bum—and could not be trusted to be around people. I began to isolate. I wanted to be LEFT ALONE.

There are long stretches of time that are very hazy. I know I truly became emotionally ill. Life was a total commitment to that bottle. All was lost and I was hopeless. The respect of my husband and my children was completely eroded. The alcohol, and the consuming need for it, clouded all awareness of this. Denial sank deep.

I woke up each morning and checked the closet to make sure my husband had not left me. When I saw his things were still there, relief washed over me. I also told myself that he still loved me and wanted me. After all, if he stayed this long, he'll stay no matter what. Therefore, I felt vindicated—and affirmed to be bad again.

I convinced myself that all was O.K. A fifth a day, at least, became normal. The summer of 1989, I gave myself over to the devil. I knew I needed my fix each day. That's life; it's how I am; I need it; and if people didn't like it—tough.

Sometimes the fifth was finished too early in the day and I would just get in the car and drive to get another one. I certainly wasn't one of those DUI people you read about in the papers—I was a very careful driver.

I avoided friends, pulled away from family, did not look at mirrors, and avoided any memories of my dad. I disappeared into the black.

Chapter 7

Intervention Day

In the back of my mind, I wondered how long I would get away with this. I really thought I would die in my sleep because my body was acting very strangely now.

It all went unspoken, but I knew my family "knew."

It was my daughter, Carolyn, who made the first contact with a counseling center to get help. Behind my back, an intervention was arranged. I sensed that something was up because my husband started to act differently. I wondered if he was having an affair. Of course, instead of thinking "who could blame him?" I thought "what a rat! If he is, he can just go away and leave me alone."

My answer to thinking "they" might be planning on a confrontation or trying to get me to shape-up was to drink even more. I anticipated the day I might be forced to cut back—so I made sure I always had plenty on hand.

My husband knew me well enough that he told me the truth the night before the intervention was to take place. I was furious and humiliated when I realized all this damn counseling had been going on behind my back. I know my dark side sensed a real threat to my privacy and my independence. How dare they! I was so angry!

My husband also had fought very hard to have immediate family, only, involved. The counselors want everyone close to you to be present. My husband knew I would have run—and he was so right. I know I would not be here today if that had happened!

As it was, the intervention day was awful. My mother looked so uncomfortable and hurt. My husband was a wreck. I felt Carolyn was in her glory. At last she could tell me off and have people listen to her and affirm her.

I closed my armor in tight around me and sat there stone-faced and agreed with everything they said. I sat and listened to a list of what they had all seen and felt as a result of my behavior. I cannot remember all that was said (I tuned a lot out). I did get a sense of the real pain and heartbreak I had been causing these dear and wonderful people. I knew all they said was absolutely true. But they didn't begin to to come close to the disgust and hate I felt for myself.

The counselor really pushed to have me admitted to the hospital right then and there. My pride won out and I absolutely refused. (Everyone would know—I would have to quit my job, my church,

INTERVENTION DAY

the yacht club, everything!)

I did compromise and agree to begin outpatient counseling the following day. My husband and I took a long walk in the park after this "intervention." He was so sorry I had to be put through the shame of it all, but he encouraged me to go ahead and try to get some help. He was so loving and kind. He told me how upset both of my daughters were over how my life was, and how much they loved me. So, I agreed to begin "treatment."

Chapter 8

The First Step—Surrender!

There was an immediate plus as treatment began—something I was surprised that I liked. I trusted the lady who became my counselor and found I could be open with her. These sessions took place in a lovely, private, women's clinic and I felt very sheltered and special. I found out I could actually get through a day without drinking. I was so relieved and so proud of myself.

I had heard how difficult recovery is and I felt lucky this came so easily. I knew I really had a problem, and mainly, it was lack of control and willpower. I came to believe I had a chance at being ladylike and "good" again. Also—very important—no one would have to know I was the "A" word. My family was so proud of me. I could see the relief and happiness on their faces.

After four weeks, I looked better, felt better, and could think straight. A huge load had been lifted off me. I felt strong and intelligent and back in

THE FIRST STEP—SURRENDER!

control for the first time in many years. I came to realize I could control my drinking. A glass of wine or a mixed drink now and then was no big deal.

However, I was careful not to let anyone know, because I really liked how happy everyone was with me. I kept telling the counselor the things I knew she wanted to hear. Also, I had started to attend a few AA meetings—especially those just for women. (I had tried meetings once before on my own about a year before. I went to one meeting that had just started and as I opened the door 30 men turned and looked at me. I had mistakenly walked into a men's only meeting. I turned and ran and never went back). I didn't feel the meetings were the place for me even now, but I went because everyone expected me to go.

I became "Miss AA" for several weeks—going to meetings and lying to my family and the counselor. I felt more and more like a phony and a hypocrite. I even spoke up at a few of the meetings and shared how good it felt to be sane and sober.

Very gradually, I "slipped" more and more. Soon I was carrying that pint in my purse again. No one said anything. One night my husband found me passed out cold on the bathroom floor and my counselor was called. I was so mad at myself for getting caught and so mad at my family for squealing.

I now had to face the fact that I was not only a derelict mess, but even AA couldn't help me. I considered very seriously that I was going to die from the effects of all this liquor and nothing and no one could help me. I was scared.

The counselor insisted that I enter a treatment center. I would go every day after work, and on the weekends, to a full fledged hospital based treatment center. This was a place that advertised frequently on television—a place I dreaded and tried to turn the conversation away from whenever the commercials came on. I felt like such a total failure. I called my husband in tears (and crying is something I did not do very often). I told him I felt so awful and the last place I wanted to go was that hospital. His answer to me was: "You don't have to go. Somehow we will work this out if you don't go. Everything will be okay, and I love you." I said; "I think I'll go."

I drove downtown to the inner city hospital treatment center. This was the one place I had dreaded for years. I was afaid. How I wished I could just undo the past six or more years of my life. I was shaking and needed a drink. How had my life ever gotten into such a mess?

I walked up the steps and as I stood before the doors I made myself a solemn from-the-heart promise. I would do whatever they told me to do. I would not lie, I would not cheat. I would absolutely follow what was suggested to me—at least for awhile. I was taking this step voluntarily; after all, it's not jail. I was free to walk out. But for now I would give it a try.

All I could really do was pray. It was a gut-wrenching feeling and a prayer of desperation. I just said: "God, I do not have a clue what is happening.

THE FIRST STEP—SURRENDER!

I need Your help. I will do whatever You guide me to do."

I realize (now) that what I did in those first moments was take (for the first time), a "first step." I surrendered.

The first step says "admit that we were powerless over alcohol and our lives had become unmanageable." Ah, yes—unmanageable. I certainly had that part. But powerless? That is much harder to think about. I am strong—and I do not want to learn how to be weak, that's just stupid—so what does powerless mean?

I walked into a room full of people from every background and race. I was stiff and scared. I was at home.

I felt a closeness with the people there. That first night I listened to the biggest, blackest, loudest man tell a horror story of drinking and drugging. Rather than feel repulsed or superior, I found myself nodding and understanding just what he was talking about, and feeling.

We ate dinner there as a group, and people laughed and joked and seemed so at ease with one another. I wondered at their casualness. I was so rigid and afraid. What was there to smile about? How in the world was I ever going to relax and have fun again? No partying, no couple of drinks to unwind. What a bore life was going to become. But life now was so swampy and black. Nothing made sense.

Chapter 9

The Disease Screams

The second evening of treatment, we discussed the "elevator of addiction." The counselor said, "it goes one way—down. The lowest possible point is death. Your own personal bottom is where you decide to get off—stop drinking—and head back up." I thought, well, I'm lucky, I'm not nearly as bad off as some people. I am a "high-bottom." As we went through the list of symptoms and feelings, both physical and mental, I took an honest look at myself. I faced the truth. I was at a very LOW bottom, and darned lucky to be alive!

The sessions were intense and the counselors were wonderful. The third evening, we went to a lecture, and when the speaker walked in, he said; "Hi, I'm Father Ray and I'm a Catholic priest, and I'm an alcoholic." I thought—he's lying. They paid him to come in and pretend because they know I'm Catholic. When Father told his story, I knew better. This man had lived through hell. Yet, here he was, healthy, happy and productive. The "program" worked for him.

THE DISEASE SCREAMS 37

I hung around afterward, waiting to talk to him alone. I asked him, "how does a good little Catholic girl, who *knows better,* ever get forgiven for all the hurt she has caused and all the wrong she has done?"

The first weekend home was HELL. I know now I should have been in de-tox, but I toughed it out on my own. I thought I would die from the physical and mental withdrawal. This was different from the other time. I had made myself a promise, and I was the one who would know if I cheated. I knew the option of a drink was closed for me and I felt crazy.

But Monday came and I went to the session and I felt so proud of myself, and so grateful for having found the strengh to hang in there. I had a little tiny feeling of hope—a feeling I had totally forgotten.

Those four weeks of daily treatment changed my life. I learned so much about me. I would come home at night exhausted from the emotional and physical strain. I slept like a baby for the first time in years.

They told me the most important part of recovery was going to meetings. Well, I went to a lot of them. And I hated them. I still felt they were dumb and I could not relate in any way. But I kept going because the counselors insisted it was the only way and I had agreed to try just what they said. Different people came in to share their stories with us in the sessions. I heard a recurring tale. Without exception, anyone who spoke of "slipping," or going out drinking again, said it was because they first stopped going to meetings. Also, the counselors there were themselves recovering people and even they went to meetings. That impressed me—so I kept going to meetings.

About four weeks into this "program," I was having a very rough Saturday. Imagine! Four weeks without drinking. It felt good, but I was feeling the familiar "antsy" feeling again and it scared me. I looked in my directory and found a noon meeting. I went to it and while I can't say I came away thrilled or anything, the weekend went better. Things were easier and my focus was on staying "well." That's when it hit me: "oh, that's how meetings work." No "high" or anything, just getting through the day was easier.

Those weeks were so hard. But everyone at the center kept saying things would get better. And things did get better. Little by little I could feel myself improving. And I heard so many horror stories of people going "back out" to the pain and misery. I was scared of a relapse. I vowed to try my best never to return to the mess I had been.

I read everything I could get my hands on. One of the most helpful books read was "Under the Influence" by Dr. James R. Milam and Katherine Ketcham. I was especially helped by the following, taken from that book:

"In the early stages of alcoholism, the alcoholic is not sick, in pain or visibly abormal. In fact, the early, adaptive stage of alcoholism appears to be marked by the opposite of the disease—for the alcoholic is blessed with a supernormal ability to tolerate alcohol and enjoy it.

"The improvement of function is tragic because the alcoholic has little or no warning of the deterio-

THE DISEASE SCREAMS

ration inevitably to follow. His disease begins long before he behaves or thinks like an alcoholic."

And this struck me most of all: "THE ALCOHOLIC IS MOST SICK, NOT WHEN HE DRINKS, BUT WHEN HE STOPS. The addicted cells will suddenly be thrown into a state of acute distress. They have become unable to function without alcohol."

In other words, I learned that this state I was in was not some moral decay, not some weakness, but a sickness that had snuck up on me. The biggest symptom of this disease is the denial of it. The more someone tells you that you have a problem, the more you do not believe it. And when you tell yourself you have a problem, THE DISEASE SCREAMS. It is protecting itself. Those addicted cells will do whatever it takes to make sure they get their regular fix. Oh! It is an ugly disease. I started carrying this book in my purse instead of a bottle!

After awhile, I stopped trying to analyze everything. I had spent so much time trying to figure out "why me," and going through my family tree questioning, groping for answers. I quit beating myself up quite so much and just accepted that this *is* me. I don't know the *how's* and *why's*, just try to deal with it day by day.

When my four weeks ended, I entered an aftercare program that met once a week for eight weeks. At the end of those eight weeks, I felt real fear of leaving the center. So, I did go back as a volunteer to share "my story" the way others had come in and shared those first few days for me.

At first it felt funny to tell total strangers about myself and act like an "expert." But when I looked at some of the faces, I saw myself reflected back. I remembered how it felt to have a pregnant daughter and no one at all to share my feelings with. I remembered that first night when I walked into that center and how scared I had felt. At least here I felt I could help someone. The haunted frightened look I saw in their eyes was the same I had seen in my own mirror (but hadn't seen in several weeks). It felt so good. And it felt so scary—such a reminder of what I did not want to return to.

Whenever I shared "my story" and got to the part about hating meetings, I would often see heads nod. I knew then I had their interest.

I know what deep denial is. I know what anger and disgust is. I could relate to just what these people were feeling. All I have to offer is my own story and perhaps a little hope. If I can get better, anyone can get better. I had proved to myself I could not do this alone. And these people couldn't either. Their lives had reached the unmanageable point, too, or they certainly wouldn't be in a drug treatment center. Some could just pass it off as bad luck or bad breaks, but sooner or later, if you live long enough, you come to the realization that this is serious and you reach out for help. Some of the stories I heard, the pain and destruction, were just unbelievable.

Quite early in recovery I got *angry* at the disease. I did not want this *illness* that I was still having trouble calling an illness. I did not want to be in recovery;

THE DISEASE SCREAMS 41

I just wanted to be normal. This is so hard. And I don't want to fail either.

When in my life did I cross the line from normalcy to screaming and agonizing dependency? I know now the enemy is not a glass of wine or beer, or a party surrounded by drinkers. It isn't me, it is the "disease," this "thing" I have. I began to envision it as an actual "thing"—a vulture-like creature hovering nearby. I can keep it quiet and calm. But if I let my guard down, if I have the slightest thought of a drink, this vulture starts to stir, ruffle its feathers, and get a gleam in it's eye. This imagery helped me and made things a little easier.

There is a stereotype attached to women who are alcoholics. We are assumed to be immoral, sleeping around, fools, and guilty of a lot of trampy behavior. I know, because I had always judged them this way—looking down on other women I had seen acting sloppy-drunk, in my mind thinking how low-life and ridiculous they seemed.

I took a good hard look at my father, too. Had he lived, would he have ever found his way to help? He was a victim, too, and I was just beginning to understand a little of what he must have gone through. It took a while before I began to forgive myself at all. It seemed like a cop-out to blame my darkness on a disease—as though I was not responsible for my own actions. I realized (Father Ray had been right), I had a choice. I could stay in my guilt and remorse or I could stop kicking myself and cringing at all my mistakes, and move on.

It wasn't easy. In fact, to this day, I still glance back and shake my head at my actions. I want to hide under the covers and never come out. I behaved so badly and my thoughts were so gross.

I can only deal with the *now*. My amends are in the present with a very limited look at the future. I can welcome some of the reminders of the past, because they tell me what I can easily return to.

I took out notes and letters my daughters wrote to me back when I was drinking, begging me to quit. My Beth wrote: "I can't squeeze any tears out anymore, but they are making my heart hurt. I lay awake all night and am so scared." I put her through that. The only way I can make amends is to stay sober, working the 12 steps and making my life good for myself and those around me. The sparkle in her eyes now is so loving and rewarding. I am so blessed!

Around the three month mark (such a miracle—90 days without a drink!), I woke up one morning and felt peace and calm. I was just breathing. I was content just to be. No churning thoughts, no knot in my stomach. It was a physical and emotional moment. This was the morning that the fear lifted. Imagine, this is how normal people are every day. I had not felt this way since I was a little girl. Some people would have no idea what I am talking about, but believe me, it was a wonderful feeling. I was filled with gratitude, joy and humility. I can really be O.K. if I just stay on the right path.

THE DISEASE SCREAMS

+ + + POSITIVELY NEGATIVE − − −

We drank for joy
 and became miserable.
We drank for sociability
 and became argumentative.
We drank for sophistication
 and became obnoxious.
We drank for friendship
 and made enemies.
We drank for sleep
 and awakened exhausted.
We drank for strength
 and felt weak.
We drank to feel exhilaration
 and ended up depressed.
We drank for "medicinal purposes"
 and acquired health problems.
We drank to get calmed down
 and ended up with the shakes.
We drank for confidence
 and became afraid.
We drank to make conversation flow more easily
 and the words came out slurred
 and incoherent.
We drank to diminish our problems
 and saw them multiply.
We drank to feel heavenly
 and ended up feeling like hell.
We drank to cope with life
 and invited death.

Chapter 10

Another Test

On Labor Day weekend of 1990, I was shopping at the Mall, feeling fit and healthy. It was a good day. I had been sober for 10 months and things were definitely better. Out of nowhere I was hit with the need for a drink like I had not felt since the beginning. It slammed me.

I thought of the State Liquor Store across the street from the Mall, the place where I had bought many a bottle of Vodka in the past. In my minds eye, I could see the door of the store and the sign above the door. I knew if I could just get away from my daughter (who was with me), for a few moments, I could run across the street, get a bottle, put it in my purse, get back to my daughter, go home, and be all set. No one would know. I felt that familiar anxious and excited feeling starting, as I planned obtaining and consuming that bottle.

Through this haze of desire came the words: "think it through," "compulsions happen," "get to a meet-

ANOTHER TEST

ing," "work your program." I thought about the things I had learned and said the Serenity Prayer. I waited for the urgency to pass—and it DID! It took a few minutes, but I calmed down. I was so grateful, and so surprised by the thoughts I had just had. I hurried home, prayed, read some literature and got to a meeting that night.

The following week I shared this "test" and this compulsion I had experienced with my group at the hospital center. I told them that my training and learning and meetings really worked and everyone was happy for me.

After the meeting, a fellow came up to me and said, "I want to talk to you." I could see he was very emotional and upset. He told me his girlfriend of many years had joined the program six months ago. Her family and friends were so happy for her; she seemed to be doing very well. One day she went shopping, with her daughter, at the same Mall where I had been. She must have had an overwhelming compulsion for a drink. She separated herself from her daughter and ran across the street (to the SAME State Liquor Store I had seen in my mind), and bought herself a bottle of Scotch.

She never made it back to the Mall. Running across the street, she was hit by a car and killed instantly.

I was numb as this man shared his story with me. This lady died with a bottle of Scotch in her purse, a victim of the disease and compulsion. I never met this lady. I don't even know her name. But I will never forget her. This lady has had more of an impact on my recovery than any other person. That could have been me. Whenever I think of her, I become more determined to stay strong, one minute to the next, one day at a time.

The above story is even more tragic than stated. While I was in the process of writing this book, I stopped in to visit my counselor and told her of the book and that I was including the story of the lady killed by the car while crossing the street. It turned out that my counselor knew the gal, and the part of the story I hadn't known.

She said that the woman (and I still don't know her name), at the time of her death, was out on bail, awaiting trial for killing two little children while she was driving drunk. What total pain she must have been in! How she must have wanted to "drown" it, to numb it! Perhaps her death could even have been a suicide. She was certainly a victim of this ugly disease. And her family! What hell this must have been for them.

Recently, I shared this entire story at an AA meeting. The anointing was awesome. We all just sat looking at one another, sad, and nodding our understanding of the pain involved.

My prayer life at this time was at the baby stage. I could recite a lot of prayers and sing a lot of beautiful, spiritual songs, but MY prayer—the from-the-heart-prayers, were terribly limited. I said the Serenity Prayer over and over each day. Sometimes all I could say was "God, serenity," or "God, help." "Thank you, God," "Stay with me, God. God... God..."

ANOTHER TEST

As my days went on, sometimes I could add quite a bit, other days, I just kept up a sort of chant, begging, grateful, pleading, praising—depending on what was happening that day. I started to feel differently toward God, like maybe He actually did love me; that I wasn't so bad after all. It was a good feeling, and I slowly found my prayer life growing and deepening. That took months, though, and for a long time I was like a little child. I found a song to sing that helped:

> Like a little child, Jesus told me to come,
>   and the Father lifts me up, up to Heaven,
>   up to home...
> Father lift me up, Alleluia, holy is your name,
> Father lift me up, Alleluia, holy is your name.
> If I die to self, Jesus told me I would live,
> Glorified with Jesus, I want to be...
> Jesus lift me up, Alleluia, holy is your name...
> Jesus lift me up Alleluia, holy is your name.

I especially liked the part about dying to self. As I pull up, out of my selfishness, it becomes easier to let God in. I sense this light now, and this "presence." I would have told you this was impossible just a short time ago. Now it's very close and very real.

At the AA meetings I attended, everyone was very careful in talking about God. No belief system is put upon anyone there and they are open to all. I began to see though, that the meetings are deeply spiritual. I would hear tough, rugged looking guys who could probably be pretty scary, talk at the meetings about someone who really made them furious, and instead of acting on their anger, they said a prayer for that person. Or if not a prayer for the person, they said the serenity prayer for themselves.

Over and over, I saw and heard evidence of God working in these people's lives. They didn't say God (sometime they said "Higher Power"), but to me it was this new God I was coming to know in a real way. I would hear a horror story and have to hide a smile with my hand as I heard where the story was leading—to growth, to love, to acceptance of self and others. And once again, I would feel filled with gratitude. I'm so blessed that I can see and understand what is happening.

I can remember that after attending lots of meetings, I finally got up the courage to speak from the heart. Oh, I had spouted off at meetings in the past, but it was to say what I thought others wanted to hear. Actually, I had wanted a standing ovation—I wanted to say something so profound that people would not ever forget what was said or who said it. When I did share something really honest and personal, one of the people sitting next to me said, "Thanks, I really liked what you said. I know just what you mean." And I thought, "Really? I actually had an idea that could help someone else in pain?" Amazing!

I learned to stop "comparison" living. Actually, I hadn't spent too much time comparing myself to others, but to what *I thought I should be*. I realize now I am not the center of it all, and I have no control over anyone's actions, thoughts or feelings, just my own. I am learning to be really content with that. In fact, I get angry very seldom now, and not because I am stuffing it. I am genuinely "stepping back."

"Lord of the Past"
Every harsh word spoken,
Every promise ever broken to me,
Total recall,
Data in the memory.
Every tear that has washed my face,
Every moment of disgrace that I have known,
Every time I've ever felt alone.
Lord of the here and now,
Lord of the come-what-may,
I want to believe somehow,
That you can heal these wounds of yesterday.
So now I'm asking you,
Do what you want to do,
Be the Lord of the past,
Oh, how I want you to.
Be the Lord of the past.

All the chances I let slip by,
All the dreams that I let die in vain,
Afraid of failure and afraid of pain.
Every tear that has washed my face,
Every moment of disgrace that I have known,
Every time I've ever felt alone.
Lord of the here and now,

I AM NEW ONE

Lord of the come-what-may,
I want to believe somehow,
You can redeem these things so far away...
Well, I picked up all these pieces,
And I built a strong deception,
And I locked myself inside of it,
For my own protection.
And I sit alone inside myself,
And curse my company,
For the thing that has kept me alive so long,
Now is killing me.

And as sure as the sun rose this morning,
and the man in the moon hides his face at
night,
I lay myself down on my bed,
And I pray this prayer inside my head...
Lord of the here and now,
Lord of the come-what-may,
You can do anything,
Be the Lord of my past.

Chapter 11

I Have Learned

Once you've been an alcoholic, you have lost your innocence. It's like losing your virginity; you can't turn back. When you have been to the blackest part of your soul, and you've had to face what is so black and ugly there, you are never quite the same again. The purity is gone; the innocence is gone.

I have seen a blackness and an ugliness I could never (and would never) put into words to anyone.

But it was there, and I am a composite of all I have thought, said, felt, or done in my life. So I know that component is there too, a part of me. True, I have shut the door on it, but little cracks of black still slip through once in a while. Recovery is a process for me—not an event. Each glimpse of the blackness is a little less crushing, a little less frightening.

Just a few weeks ago, I was in the grocery store—in a hurry with lots on my mind. As I walked through the wine section, suddenly my mouth began to water.

The saliva actually came out of the corners of my mouth! I stopped dead still in the aisle and asked myself, "where in the world did this come from?" I had no thought of drinking, no desire for this stuff, and no intention of buying any liquor, so what was going on? Then I thought: "Oh, thank You God! Thank You for this reminder that I am a recovering person. I still have alcoholism. Thank You for this little nudge, this little reminder. The blackness is still hovering nearby. And most of all, thank You, thank You for the grace and the strength to recognize this for what it is—just a reminder. Not a failure, not a mistake. Most importantly, thank You for the awareness that I can shrug this off—keep moving—not dwell on this! Instead of being all upset that I had this episode, I can view it as a positive little happening. (Also, thanks for the thought that I had better get to a meeting—tonight!)"

The shift from addiction to recovery is a spiritual transformation.

Your worst sinfulness and brokenness—the total complete bottom—is your greatest blessing. It's what breaks you open. No more hiding, denial, pretending, or ignoring. Now you are raw and open, and the grace can slip in and healing can begin.

The image comes to me of a hard-boiled egg, cracked and peeling. When the shell is all gone, it is smooth and pure, soft and vulnerable. That is the bottom—except of course the skin is not pure, it is bruised and bloody—but it is definitely raw and vulnerable.

I HAVE LEARNED

And if this egg is merely cracked or if the shell is not totally gone, then a part of the defenses still remain, pieces of denial are left, and total acceptance and healing cannot begin because the shell will start to heal itself, not what is inside!

This bottom is a cursed place and a blessed place. It is a gift. It is life itself from a God Who has not given up, and Who has loved us through the blackness. It is during the darkness, at the lowest possible point, that His grace burns brightest.

Those first months of recovery I was in a "pink fog," so thick I didn't even know it was a fog until it started to lift. I can see now that the fog really protected me. All the reality of how insane my thinking had been did not flood in all at once. It came gradually, as I was able to bear it.

I found a twelve step group I really liked. I came to look forward to sharing with these people. I credit their wisdom with getting me through a lot of rough spots. The people were down to earth and filled with a lot of wisdom and common sense. I felt at home.

My recovery has really been a joyful experience. Oh, the first few months were not joyful, they were hell. But everyone kept saying, it will get better if you stick with it. And they were right. I can live a full, rich, productive life, free from the prison I had been in.

Often I ask, "Why me?" I have no answer to that. I just know that sobriety is my top priority. I put being sober first in my life and guard against all threats against it. I pray unceasingly every day, and try to stay strong spiritually.

I realize the bottom I hit was a gift from God. God's ways are so upside down from our ways. In littleness, we become great. In humility is great strength. The weakness, our cross, is our greatest opportunity to give glory to God. But until someone feels this for himself, these are just words.

When I was at the darkest, when I was the most sick, God was there. The first bottom I hit was mental. I was loosing my memory; I was becoming quite insane. The second bottom was physical. My body had built up an allergy to the one thing I needed most. I had constant diarrhea. My throat burned. My insides were mushy. The third bottom I hit, and the one that did the most damage to this human being, was spiritual. I truly feel I have glimpsed Hell. It is devastatingly ugly.

And, when I saw Hell, I looked up. And there was grace.

Chapter 12

And The Grace Flowed

In recovery, staying sober must be the priority of your life. YOU make the decision. YOU decide. Will this day be spent sober and productive, or will it be a day you take a drink and return to all the heartache and misery?

You do not have to live that way. You may feel the pull, and think you can't make it without a drink. YES, YOU CAN.

You may think to hell with it—no one cares and no one will know—YOU WILL KNOW.

There are a thousand excuses to drink. There is no reason. The Big Book says this disease is cunning, baffling and powerful. Sometimes that ugly vulture sitting on my shoulder gets quiet. I can even forget he's there. Then I hear a little voice softly say: "You're strong now. You can handle anything. No one can tell you you can't drink anymore, you could handle it. One drink after all this time won't hurt. Who's to know. Don't let anyone boss you, especially after this rough day you've had."

When my thoughts even hint toward that direction, I recognize the disease talking. It wants me back. I pray, get to a meeting. I take action to get myself back on good spiritual and emotional footing. God provides the direction and I provide the action. And it works!

True freedom for me is being without a chain; walking with, partying with, relaxing with friends and family—in any setting; being around drinking and ignoring it, truly not wanting it. Serenity, peace, happiness!

When I sank into that darkness, my husband had found a way to deal with the loss of his wife, friend and companion. He turned to "religion." I could see this happening in a vauge and fuzzy way. All I knew was he was occupied and left me alone.

One evening some friends visited and talked about a miracle that was taking place over in Europe—sort of a modern day Fatima. When they left, they left behind a newspaper written by an American journalist, Wayne Weible. My husband sat down and read this paper cover to cover. From that moment, he was changed.

He believed immediately that the Blessed Virgin Mary was appearing to six young children in Yugoslavia. He ordered video tapes that showed the village of Medjugorje and the six kids as they visited with and prayed with Mary. This miracle had been occuring since June 25, 1981.

I saw my husband begin to change. He started to carry a rosary everywhere he went. I would wake

AND THE GRACE FLOWED 57

up in the middle of the night and find him praying. He started to talk about this phenomenon everywhere he went.

It was shortly after he threw himself into this new spiritual and prayerful life, that I went through "treatment" and began the journey of recovery. I know it was more than a coincidence that grace entered my life as he began to pray for me.

As I progressed in "finding myself" and working on being "normal," my husband became more engrossed in finding out more about this miracle of God that was happening in Europe. I remained cynical and somewhat indifferent, although I was curious and would listen to the things he was learning. He sought out people who had traveled to Medjugorje and decided we were going to travel to this country and see for ourselves what was going on.

I was beginning to feel pretty good, although I was still a little shaky. I decided to go along however, and by a miracle, we came into some money that would allow us to make the trip. I thought I had better go to keep an eye on him, because I was afraid he was going to go off the deep end and become a fanatic. I was a real skeptic and knew I could prevent us from being duped. I also thought it would be nice to tell people I was traveling to Europe—it sounded so sophisticated. Lastly, it was in the back of my mind that if something really was "happening" over there, I wanted to be a part of it.

On June 21, 1991, we left for Medjugorje. We traveled with a group and a guide. We quickly realized this was not going to be a vacation, but a prayerful pilgrimage. There were two Catholic priests in our group and they said Mass in the airport in New York before we left.

The people in our group seemed so holy, and way above my head spiritually. When someone lost their luggage and found it again, they said: "Our Lady found our luggage." When the plane was a little late in taking off, they said "Our Lady wants the plane to leave a little later." Everything was, "Our Lady... Our Lady"...I thought, "I don't get it!"

The trip was long and exhausting. It was scary coming into a communisty country. Soldiers were at the gates at the airports, and they seemed very threatening. There had been troubles reported in the area and we took a very round-about way to get to the village. The trip to get into the mountains by bus was beautiful. The Adriatic sea was blue and sparkling. We prayed the Rosary, and sang songs, and prepared ourselves for a real retreat. This began to seem like a true pilgrimage and a sacrifice. We were so tired.

As we finally came into the village that first evening, everyone on the bus became very excited. My husband could hardly believe we had arrived. At last, all the pictures and videos were "real." I thought: "What am I doing here?"

It was 10:00 p.m. when we arrived, exhausted and out of it from lack of sleep and the grueling trip. We stayed in a home in the village, and the family had waited up for us with smiles of welcome and a meal of hot soup and fresh bread. Before we went to bed, our guide told us: "Not one of you got here by accident. You were called. Our Lord and Our Lady brought you here for a reason. You have answered the call and can now pray, fast and enter your journey." I thought, "God, why would You call me here? What do You want of me? I am not worthy to be here around these holy people. They don't know how sinful and ugly I have been. Please show me what You want."

We awoke our first morning in Medjugorje to the sound of the rooster crowing in the back yard, and the buses coming down the narrow paths bringing more and more pilgrims. Before breakfast, we walked to the village to see the church. The church of St. James is located in the center of the village and all roads lead to it. Before Our Lady began appearing in 1981, there had been 400 families in this area. Yet, they had built a huge church. We heard Mass coming from loudspeakers located around the outside of the church. People were kneeling on the steps praying and the church was packed. All around the church, lines were forming with people waiting to go to confession. The sacrament was available in all languages. It was all prayerful and peaceful—especially if you turned your back to the ring of taxi cabs and commercialism that surrounded the church.

We returned to the house to share breakfast with our group. Our hostess, Stepha, was a very good cook. The food was simple but very good. Stepha and her family had added on to their home, as many other villagers had, to help accommodate the huge crowds that came to the village. In the early years of the apparitions, they had slept in the hay in the barn and turned their own living rooms and bedrooms over to the pilgrims. This village had truly been touched by a spirit of loving and sharing. Their generosity made it possible for pilgrims to attend Mass, climb the mountain, or just go off alone to pray without being distracted by anything. We surely invaded their privacy, but when we cut through their back yards to get to Mass and walked by their cows and goats tethered in the grass, they just smiled and waved. They were glad we were there—in this oasis of prayer.

Our first excursion was a climb up Apparition Hill. This was located ten minutes away from the house. We took a dirt path, past grape vineyards and hay stacks, to the bottom of a rocky hill. There were people walking past us, praying the Rosary and speaking in a variety of languages. The little mountain we were to climb was covered with rocks, worn smooth from the foot traffic of thousands of pilgrims. Hundreds of homemade crosses, some covered with pictures of children and loved ones, had been left behind. Our guide told us that a young pilgrim, a drug addict from the United States, had come to this mountain and experienced a powerful conversion. He had stayed in Medjugorje and as part of his service came along the mountain every few weeks and removed the crosses and mementos people had left. So many millions have come to this little spot that it would not be possible to walk it if someone did not do this.

When we got to the place on the hill marked by a large cross with hundreds of candles burning, we knew we were at the place where Mary had first appeared to the visionaries on June 24, 1981. It was quiet and peaceful, and everyone was praying. Our group went off to the side and as a part of our prayer, we all stated the reasons or intentions that had brought us there. Two priests were traveling with us. One came as an active priest; he would be celebrating Mass that evening. The other priest came "incognito." He wanted to experience Medjugorje as a pilgrim. We had a husband and wife traveling with four of their seven children. We had a mother traveling with three of her fifteen grown children. We had a Sister from the Dominican order, and several other couples and families. Each had come with their own unique story, wanting and expecting something different. On that mountain, our hearts began to open and we came to realize the truth of the saying, "You are called." God knows our wants and needs and He had used His Mother to call us to this holy experience.

All my life as a good little Catholic I had heard these things. None of this was new to me, but now I could see from a different perspective that God really does love me, in spite of all my failings. Just like all the silly cliche's I had heard in the AA meetings "One Day at a Time"; "Easy Does It"; things I had heard all my life had a new and relevant meaning to me.

That evening we attended the Croatian Mass. I have heard of people who have made the trip to Medjugorje and had never gone to the Croatian Mass. I think they have missed out on the whole reason for being in that village at all. The bell calling us to Mass seemed like it made the entire village move toward the church. Everyone was anxious to get there and pray. At 6:00 p.m., the Rosary began. We sat outside on the benches surrounding the gazebo. Mass had been moved outside because the church is not large enough to accommodate the crowds. Father would say the Rosary in Croatian and was answered back in many different languages.

At exactly twenty minutes to seven, all stopped and there was total silence—as that is the time when Our Lady was meeting with the visionaries. After a few moments, the Rosary resumed. About 7:00, Mass began, in Croatian. The gospel was read in seven different languages. The homily was given by one of the parish priests. He spoke in Croatian—for about an hour. And no one minded; they just sat and listened. The singing was simple and sweet, the choir very nice, and everyone joined in, for several songs were familiar. The order of the Mass is the same everywhere, so it was easy to follow what was going on. After Mass, there was a beautiful Benediction. I had not been to a benediction in a long time and I had forgotten how powerful and special it can be. Following Benediction, Father blessed all the sick people and then there was a general blessing of all religious articles. The sun had long set on us before all was finished, about 9:30. Three and one half hours,

AND THE GRACE FLOWED 63

and no one was in a rush to leave!

That first night, after Mass, our group met and got to visit with the visionary, Ivanka. She was very sweet, and so ordinary. No different than anyone else and putting on no "airs." We stared at her, trying to imagine what it must be like to see the Mother of God. She just smiled and said, "What is important is that you live the messages."

The next day was June 24th, the Feast of St. John the Baptist, and the 10th anniversary day of when Our Lady had first appeared to the children. My husband and I were happy because our parish is St. John the Baptist. We were surprised to learn what a major feast day St. John's is in Yugoslavia. There are big celebrations. The hostess of our house planned champagne and a special meal, putting out her good linens. But early that morning, our group was climbing the mountain. The temperature was close to 100 during the day, so we wanted to beat the heat. We gathered at the foot of Mt. Podbrdo at 5:00 a.m. The stations of the cross are said along the climb. We prayed and sang and stopped at each station to read a prayer and meditate on the passion of Jesus. The air was hot and the sky was clear. As we climbed, we could look back and see the village below us, and the church—the center of everything.

Some of the native Croatian ladies were making the climb alongside us, and they were barefoot. It was unbelievable. This mountain was rocky and rugged, and covered with sharp stones and brambles. Yet as a sacrifice to God, they were barefoot! It humbled all of us. When we reached the very top of the mountain we saw the thirty foot high cement cross. The view was breathtaking. We remained a long time, taking pictures and praying. I remember thinking—boy if the people back home could see me now. It's 9:00 in the morning and I've just climbed to the top of this mountain. Not only that, but I was at church last night, praying for three and a half hours, and loving it! Wow! Seeing this mountain and these people through the eyes of a recovering addict was so humbling and moving. I cried a lot that day.

Mass that evening was a repeat of the night before. Medjugorje is Rosary, Mass, Rosary, Mass, climb a mountain, Rosary, Mass. And happy, peacefilled people. I never saw Mary, and I never experienced the sun spinning, which many claimed to see. But I did feel my heart beginning to open and change, and it was a good feeling.

The next morning, our group took a short walk to the home of Maria. Maria is the visionary who is given Our Lady's message for the world on the 25th of each month. Maria was standing outside on her front porch, speaking in Italian to a large group of tourists. I could pick out just a few words of her conversation—bread and water, television, pleasures—and I knew she was talking about fasting. Our Lady asks for fasting. She asks us to fast on Wednesday and Fridays. Bread and water only.

I left the group and walked to Apparition Hill alone. I know Our Lady has called us to fast and pray. I thought: "I am a failure, because I can't fast, and my prayer life is not so good." I sat quietly for a long time. Then the thought quietly came to me: Wait a minute! I do fast. I fast every day from the one thing my body craves most. And the only way I maintain this fast is through God's grace. I offer this as my gift to God every day, over and over. And yet, this is not something I am giving to God, it is something God is giving to me!

What a grace to be given this special channel to offer up to God, as He showers down on me. I prayed then, and I pray now, for the strength to maintain my fast. To pray with my entire body. Let this be my top priority. Sobriety. Serenity. I felt new comfort and meaning in those simple words.

And it doesn't matter if I fail at other types of fasting. In fact, if my entire day has been the pits, if I have maintained my fast from drinking, it is a holy day!

Fasting can be little acts of mortification. Wanting a soda and taking a glass of water instead. Turning off the T.V. when your favorite program comes on. Ironing one more shirt before stopping. Saying a quick little prayer for the person who cuts you off in traffic. Not eating meat on Friday, just as your own remembrance. These kinds of things can be done with no one else knowing. This is not done for others; it is done for God. You will come to know it is being done BY God. And your soul opens just a little bit more to let in just a bit more grace. Soon it becomes routine and actually something to look forward to. Such a gift! God does not take from me. As I give to Him, He gives back to me a hundred-fold. I cannot out-give Him. The depth of His love is something we cannot begin to understand.

> *"Dear children, pray for the gift of love, for the gift of faith, for the gift of prayer, for the gift of fasting!"* (Our Lady's Message of April 17, 1986.

Chapter 13

Prayer From The Heart

Did I have to come 8,000 miles to learn this? I don't know, but I do know that this "word of knowledge" passed from my head to my heart on that little mountain.

I didn't know just how to put all this into words just yet, and I was very quiet as I rejoined our group and we walked to the Church for the Croatian Mass.

It was beastly hot with just a slight breeze. The gravel crunched underfoot as we took our seats outside. The Rosary began and as Fr. Slavko said the prayers in Croatian, he was answered in many different languages. The rhymth was right though—a wonderful cadence.

I was lost in prayer—a unique experience for me to pray so strongly from the heart. And as we continued praying, I found myself answering the Hail Mary in a language I had not ever heard, just these strange sounds coming from me—how odd! And as

I mouthed these words, I could "see" Mary and the disciples walking along trails, climbing hills, laughing and talking with one another. I could see them as if they were on a T.V. screen in front of me. This sensation did not last long, but it was so intense and so beautiful, I wanted it back. I tried to concentrate and see the scene again, but it wouldn't come back.

There was an excitement in me I had never felt before, a humming in my ears, and a glow over everything. Once again, the Mass and the prayers passed by so quickly.

We would be leaving Medjugorje the next morning and our group gathered that night after Mass for dinner and one last evening together. We had "pizza"—well, Stepha called it pizza, but it wasn't what we were used to. Anyway, we talked and laughed and sang songs. It was wonderful. Everyone's experience that week had been profound and moving.

We asked one of our priests to say a prayer before we ate our meal and he said the following:

"The Baker Woman"

A Baker Woman in her humble lodge
  received a grain of wheat from God.
For nine whole months the grain she stored
  behold the handmaid of the Lord.
Make us the bread Mary, Mary,
  make us the bread,
  we need to be fed.

The Baker Woman took the road which led
  to Bethlehem, the house of bread.

PRAYER FROM THE HEART

To kneed the dough she labored through the night
   then brought it forth about midnight.
Bake us the bread, Mary, Mary,
   bake us the Bread,
   we need to be fed.
She baked the bread for thirty years
   by the fire of her love and the salt of her tears,
By the warmth of a heart so tender and bright
   and the bread, the bread was golden brown and white.
Bring us the bread Mary, Mary,
   bring us the bread,
   we need to be fed.

After thirty years the bread was done
   it was taken to town by her only son.
The soft white bread to be given free
   to the hungry people of Galilee.
Give us the bread Mary, Mary,
   give us the bread,
   we need to be fed.

For thirty coins the bread was sold
   and a thousand teeth so cold, so cold.
Tore it to pieces on a Friday noon
   and the sun turned black—and red the moon.
Break us the bread Mary, Mary,
   break us the bread,
   we need to be fed.

But the Baker Woman's only son
   when she saw the bread so white,

The Living Bread she had brought forth in the night
   devoured as wolves might devour sheep,
   the Baker Woman began to weep.
   Weep for the bread Mary, Mary,
   weep for the bread,
   we need to be fed.

But the Baker Woman's only son
   appeared to His friends when three days had gone.
On the road to which Emmaus lead
   they knew Him in the breaking of the bread.
Lift up your head, Mary, Mary,
   lift up your head,
   for now we have been fed.

Lift up your head, Mary, Mary,
   lift up your head,
   for now we have been fed.

I went out of the house and into the fields, in the dark, when the prayer was finished. Here I had come to this little village of peasants. I had come as a cynic. I had taken what seemed to be a step backwards in a time machine, and saw people with no cars, no wealth, no big stores, no fancy clothes. I thought "wouldn't these people faint away if they saw the abundance of food and wealth we have in our country."

I thought the life here must be reminiscent of the days when Jesus and the disciples walked the earth. I had come to try and be open, and yet, I had been afraid of what would "happen" to me. I was overwhelmed with gratitude, especially for my little

Stephanie. I realized what a gift, what a grace God had given me by not allowing that abortion to happen. The guilt I had been feeling for eight years left me. I placed Steph's life at the foot of Our Lady and asked for protection for her. And, I placed my disease at the foot of the cross, and I smiled. I saw for the first time in my life the true meaning of *"my yoke is easy and my burden light."*

I am so grateful for my cross. It has made me strong, and pure, and clean. My worst nightmare is my greatest blessing. My children and my family are so precious to me. And, I want to do God's will, to be His instrument in however He might want to use me.

I didn't know it then, but I know it now; my entire outlook on life had changed. I had touched and felt the beautiful mosaic of God's plan for us, and so many pieces fell into place. I thought about my dad, and I smiled. I recalled some of the terrible things we had gone through in our family. I could remember them—but the pain was gone. I totally and unconditionally forgave him. It was lifted like a huge load off my chest. The Holy Spirit was present right there in that field. It filled my soul and changed my life forever.

Our group left for home the next morning as the moon was still shining. We were all anxious to get home, yet sad to leave this wonderful place. Our host families gave us wonderful homemade pastries to eat on the way, and packed sandwiches of fresh bread and goat cheese. How we would miss the smiling faces of these holy people! I hoped I would never forget the lessons of simplicity I learned from them.

We took a very round-about and scenic way through the mountains to Zagreb. The ride took eight hours! Never have I seen such grandeur and beauty as I saw in those mountains. It seemed like every corner we rounded was more breathtaking than the next. We passed several "checkpoints" with soldiers and guns. They just waved us on.

The folks on the bus decided to "stage" a musical—"The Sound of Music." What a fun time was had by all. Several of the younger girls put T-shirts over their heads; they were the sisters in the convent singing about Maria. We yodeled together, laughed 'till we cried, and got melancholy as we sang "Edelweiss." As we sang "Climb Every Mountain" with the mountains passing outside the bus windows, we felt very uplifted.

Everyone took a turn at the microphone on the bus and told what the trip had meant to them. Many people were in tears as they told how their hearts had opened, and how they had come closer to God.

That "joy-thing" kept rising up in my throat. I had some time to think during that ride, about all I had seen and heard on this trip. As a person in recovery I wanted to find ways to help me in my own personal recovery program. And I feel the most important thing I came away with, besides a renewed love for our Triune God, were the words of Our Lady; *"Pray from the heart."* Mary asks us to pray—every day.

She asks for the Rosary—every day. The Rosary is a difficult prayer and I had never said it except when in a group, or been "forced" to. Yet I was beginning to realize that the Rosary is actually a lesson in "right thinking." It's impossible to really pray the Rosary each day, meditate on the life, death and resurrection story of Jesus, and not be changed in the way you live your life. It gives everything a balance and perspective. It keeps you focused on goodness and love, and sacrifice and joy. And if I can mesh my prayer life, my spiritual life, with my recovery, my "program," then the practical side of living becomes easier, more productive, and in balance. My head was racing with these thoughts and with love. I felt like a new person, and like there would be many adventures ahead. I couldn't wait to get home.

When we reached the airport in Zagreb, we were told to "Hurry! Hurry!" Suddenly our guides and the people at the airport seemed frantic. They had kept the news from us that WAR had been declared in Yugoslavia during the week we were in the mountains! This made no sense! We had come from a total oasis of peace, only to see war planes flying low over the airport and armored tanks on the runways with their turrets pointed at the airport.

One attendant grabbed my arm as we were running down the hall toward the plane and said, "Please pray for us." The plane finally did leave without incident, and we were then told that the airport immediately closed after our plane left.

As we flew out of Yugoslavia airspace, my thoughts

turned to Stepha and her family, and the others who had opened their homes and their hearts to us. What would become of them? The tranquility and peace of those mountains seemed the least likely place on earth for guns and bloodshed. Yet, it was the least likely place for Our Lady to begin appearing, also. She must have been preparing her children. She must have known how very much we would need her.

I have wondered, since returning home, how our guides felt on that bus as we went the "back way" through those mountains. We had been singing and remembering a story of a family that had fled to Austria to escape an army. What an irony! I hope our actions gave them strength and courage.

Chapter 14

I Am New One

When my husband and I returned from Medjugorje, we were on fire to tell people the experiences we had on our trip. One of the very wise priests on our trip counseled us before we parted, "tread softly." The world had not changed just because we had (figuratively) seen the face of God.

It was good advice to take things slowly, and to discern the things we had learned. However, this conversion experience was not merely a "spiritual high." It was life changing. We have tried to live and spread the messages. And in recovery, I have grown so much.

I realize now that I was Baptized in the Holy Spirit on the hillside in Yugoslavia. The Holy Spirit entered my life in a new way because I had prayed, fasted, and became ready and open. I did not travel thousands of miles for this, but I sure had to come on a long, bumpy journey, to get to the point where I humbly recognized my need for God. In this humility has come such strength and such joy.

There were some doubts along the way, too. And sometimes I felt a real "presence" pulling me away from all holiness. A wise sister pointed out to me— the closer you get to Jesus, especially in the beginning of an intense spiritual journey, the harder the evil one tries to pull you away. He does not want you to do this. I bowed my head and cried, because indeed, I could see and feel that darkness tried to creep in. It was a last-ditch effort to pull me from grace. But Our Lady is too strong and prayer is too powerful! Jesus and Mary have won my heart.

Jesus had been with me every minute of my life. And I know He repeatedly knocked, pounded, kicked, gently tapped, and tried every other way of entrance into my heart. Then one day, He sent His mother.

It was in answer to her call that I turned my life around. In fact, the first days following our return home, I often forgot about Jesus and prayed to and for and with Mary. But she gradually pulled back and I was so hungry for The Word in Scripture, the Mass, and Jesus. After a month or so, I realized I had not been praying so much to Mary, that Jesus had become the number one love of my life. Mary, oh so gently, drew me to her and then turned me to Jesus. She gently pushed me—like a mother. Then as I opened and filled with Her Divine Son, she withdrew and left all the worship and glory for Him alone. What a loving and humble act this was on Our Lady's part. It made me love her so. And then, how much I love the One who sent her in the first place.

Catholics are so often criticized for their "worship" of Mary. Many times the criticism comes from priests and religious who know better. They know we honor Mary and have great devotion to her. Anyone who does "worship" Mary and gives her "powers" that are divine, is very mistaken and misguided and needs to be lovingly and firmly set straight. But those Catholics who have fallen away from devotion for Mary have missed so much. Those who consecrate their lives and vocations to her will be assisted in living holy lives.

Our Lady's messages are too simple for some—too basic. She does not "challenge" the intellect. That is why she comes to simple children, those innocents who unquestioningly love her and accept her. We do not see that those simple messages are the hardest to live. It is difficult to make time for prayer. The ways of the world keep competing. We have closed our hearts.

We do not "need" Mary to reach Heaven. But speaking for myself, I am so glad my heavenly mother saw fit to assist me in finding her Son. I don't want to think about where I might be now if this grace had not entered my life. I will be eternally grateful. I hope that people will see the light of Christ shining in me. It is there for all. God loves us so much.

Praise be Jesus and Mary, now and forever.

"DEAR CHILDREN... PRAY, PRAY, PRAY"

Message of Our Lady... *"there will be in the future, signs concerning sinners, unbelievers, alcoholics and young people. They will accept me again."*

Epilogue

As I worked on putting the finishing touches on this manuscript, I became very busy and preoccupied. I still attended prayer group and Mass and prayed throughout the day. But I stopped going to meetings. I just did not have time. There was too much to do, too much going on in my life. I also thought—I am so involved in prayer, Jesus, and the Church, that I'm fine. And I was busy, busy.

At work, though, people were really starting to annoy me. It was aggravating just to be around people. Even when I got home, things weren't going the way I thought they should. I had no thoughts of drinking, or escaping, or anything like that; I was just ticked-off at people. And I wanted to be ALONE.

One morning at work, my boss (who is in recovery) was walking past me as he moved down the hall. I turned and started to call after him. I wanted, in the worst way, to tell him—"I'm not having a good day; I think I'm losing it; what's going on?" But pride held me back and I turned around and walked away.

EPILOGUE

I returned to my desk and sat there for a minute with my head in my hands and I prayed, "God, you better help me. Something isn't right here. I need help."

It was ten minutes later, this same boss came into my office and said "Come into the conference room; I need to talk to you." I thought, "Oh, brother, what have I done wrong and what's his problem?" He said, "I'm chairman for my AA group tomorrow night and I was wondering if you would come and do a lead for us?" At first I said "no"—then I said—"wait, yes, of course I will." That night at home, while I was making a few notes and getting ready to give my lead and tell "my story" at the meeting the next night, I looked up from my desk and thought, "the darkness had gotten close again."

What a fool I had been! I had been gradually slipping and letting things get out of balance in my life. This disease is cunning, baffling, powerful—also sneaky and patient. It was just coming at me in a different direction. And God, in His loving way, answered my prayer for help. He threw me a life-line by using someone else to come to me and pull me back to meetings, the fellowship, and where I belong.

It scares me, how close I came to slipping. I turned and there was that hideous, grinning vulture sitting on my shoulder again, eyeing me with a smirk. Too darn close.

God is showing this recovering person how to stick with this process of living that I know works. Jesus is with me, every step of the way. But He is counting on me to do my share too. All praise to this loving and generous God! Creator, King, Saviour, Brother, Friend!

Each day, I am a new creation. One day at a time. I am a new child of God, a new person, given a new chance at a new and better way of life. "I AM NEW ONE."

Message from Our Lady of Medjugorje (3/25/92)

"Dear Children: Today as never before I invite you to live my messages and put them to practice in your life. I have come to you to help you and therefore I invite you to change your life because you have taken a path of misery—a path of ruin. When I told you to convert yourself, pray, fast, be reconciled—you took these messages superficially. You started to live them and then you stopped because it was difficult for you. Now, dear children, when something is good you have to persevere in the good and not think "God is not listening, He is not helping" and so you have gone away from God and from me because of your miserable interests. I wanted to create of you an oasis of peace, love and goodness. God wanted you, with your love and His help, to do miracles and thus give an example. Therefore, here is what I am saying to you—Satan is playing with you and with your souls and I cannot

help you because you are far from my heart. Therefore, pray, live my messages and then you will see the miracle of God's love in your every day life. Thank you for having responded to my call."

Credits

Prayer on page 47, "Father Lift Me Up" from:
>Maranatha Music
>P.O. Box 1396
>Costa Mesa, CA 92626

Prayer on page 49, "Lord of the Past" from:
>the album "Lord of the Past"
>words and music by Bob Barnett
>Matters of the Heart Music/ASCAP (1989) &
>>Urgent Records Co. (1989)

Medjugorje message on page 77, from the book:
>"Letters from Medjugorje"
>Wayne Weible
>pg. 125

The testimonial titled "Positively Negative"
>(Anonymous Author)

ADDITIONAL TITLES AVAILABLE
Contact The Riehle Foundation

WHY PRAYER? AND HOW TO PRAY
by Fr. René Laurentin

A brilliant yet simple look at prayer. Fr. Laurentin reminds us of the often forgotten truth: "God is the Creator; we are the created," the only existence which gives meaning to everything else.

104 pages   **$4.00**

Time for Jesus: AN HOUR WITH JESUS

Millions of people are experiencing conversion and turning to a deeper relationship with God—finding themselves drawn to Jesus' true presence in the Holy Eucharist. This booklet provides meditations for Eucharistic Adoration, or for anyone simply stopping in church to pray before the tabernacle. New, but very popular already!

120 pages   **$2.00**

THE POWER OF THE ROSARY
by Fr. Albert J. Shamon

Historical instances of how praying the rosary has been a powerful weapon for peace. Suggestions on how to meditate, and many reasons why the Rosary prayer is so powerful.

48 pages   **$2.00**

(Also available in Spanish)
El Poder Del Rosario

THE RIEHLE FOUNDATION...

The Riehle Foundation is a non-profit, tax-exempt, charitable organization that exists to produce and/or distribute Catholic material to anyone, anywhere.

The Foundation is dedicated to the Mother of God and her role in the salvation of mankind. We believe that this role has not diminished in our time, but, on the contrary has become all the more apparent in this the era of Mary as recognized by Pope John Paul II, whom we strongly support.

During the past five years the foundation has distributed over four million books, films, rosaries, bibles, etc. to individuals, parishes, and organizations all over the world. Additionally, the foundation sends materials to missions and parishes in a dozen foreign countries.

Donations forwarded to The Riehle Foundation for the materials distributed provide our sole support. We appreciate your assistance, and request your prayers.

For copies of the books listed here, or for a catalog, contact:

The Riehle Foundation
P.O. Box 7
Milford, OH 45150
513-576-0032